CHAPARRAL

Can-Am Racing Cars from Texas

Introduction by
Karl Ludvigsen

Iconografix

Iconografix
PO Box 446
Hudson, Wisconsin 54016 USA

Library of Congress Card Number: 2001135733

ISBN 1-58388-066-6

02 03 04 05 06 07 08 5 4 3 2 1

Printed in China

Cover and book design by Shawn Glidden

Copyedited by Suzie Helberg

COVER PHOTO: Jim Hall stunned the world of racing with his high-winged Chaparral 2E in 1966. He developed it into the more powerful 2G for the 1967 Can-Am racing season, as shown in this photo from the Ludvigsen Library.

Those Amazing White Cars from Texas

By Karl Ludvigsen

It seemed to be the logical next step, yet when it happened it surpassed most expectations. Making serious sports-racing cars in America started on the East Coast in the modern era with Briggs Cunningham and his magnificent cars. Wealthy sportsman Briggs was not one to see the Jaguars, Ferraris, and Allards take all the prizes. He built his own Cunninghams in Florida from 1951 through 1955, and saw them win big in America and perform with pride at Le Mans.

Next it was the West Coast's chance. Having caught the racing bug, young Lance Reventlow invested his Woolworth inheritance in the magnificent Scarab sports-racers and Grand Prix cars from 1958 through 1961. California was in the ascendancy, with Carroll Shelby taking over Reventlow's facility and creating his fabled Cobras.

Then came the rumblings from Texas. It was the turn of another region of America. John Mecom set up an impressive team that supplied winners both at Indianapolis and in the big sports-car events. There was word of strange doings at Midland, Texas. Midland has been described as where you are "when you're too far from El Paso and you can't get to Houston," a hard-working oil, cattle, and cotton town. Midland is where oil-explorer Jim Hall and oil-driller James "Hap" Sharp combined forces to design and build the astonishing Chaparral sports-racers.

I've always been fascinated by the Chaparrals; I was at Riverside testing a Scarab on the same summer day in 1961 that saw Hall shaking down his original front-engined Chaparral with its builders Dick Troutman and Tom Barnes—this book's first photographs. Later I helped introduce Hall and Sharp to Bill Mitchell at GM Styling, a connection that blossomed into a closer relationship with Chevrolet. I was at Bridgehampton in 1966 when the first winged 2Es appeared, wonderful works of art and science. Still employed by GM then, I had a few insights into the links between its Chevrolet Division and Chaparral cars.

In the late 1960s I covered the Can-Am racing series for several publications and wrote a book about the series and its cars. That gave me a chance to gain some understanding of the Chaparrals and their builders. The photographs in this book, all from the files of the Ludvigsen Library, were taken chiefly by myself, Stanley Rosenthall, Edward Eves and Max Le Grand. Other sources have been Larry Shinoda and Judy Stropus. In refreshing my recollections of the Chaparrals two books have been essential, *Can-Am* by Pete Lyons and *Chaparral* by Richard Falconer with Doug Nye.

Abilene-born James Ellis Hall was only 17 in the summer of 1953 when his parents and a sister were killed in a light-plane crash. He was the middle of two brothers, a trio who did their best to keep Condor Petroleum—their geologist father's company—alive and well. At Cal Tech Jim studied geology and then switched to mechanical engineering. With his older brother also involved in an imported-car dealership, Jim began racing cars at the age of 19. A link with the past was his chief mechanic, Red Byron, who had also wrenched for Briggs Cunningham. Hall was successful with some heavy machinery, developing a special liking for Maseratis.

With fellow enthusiasts, including the eight-years-older Hap Sharp and Ronnie Hissom, Hall invested in the aptly dubbed Rattlesnake Raceway, a pear-shaped 1.97-mile racetrack on the south side of Midland. Jim and Hap had aluminum shop buildings on their two-acre Raceway plots, which they paved between to make a common compound. Both men realized that if they wanted to gain the upper hand as sports-car racers they should build their own, something that engineering graduate Hall was already thinking about. With this as their aim they incorporated Chaparral Cars in January 1962—naming it after a fast-running Texan relation of the cuckoo and a tough western shrubbery.

Jim Hall wet his feet in car building by backing the plan of talented Californians Dick Troutman and Tom Barnes to create a Chevrolet-powered sports-racer that they saw as an evolution of the Scarab, which they'd helped build. When Hall agreed to fund their prototype they cheerfully discarded their intended name, "Riverside," to make it the first Chaparral. With all-independent suspension and its engine set well back, the Troutman-Barnes car was one of the best last front-engined sports-racers. In 1962, Jim won two races at Elkhart Lake with one of the five cars made.

"They were awfully far away," said Hall of the California builders. "It wasn't much fun having it built way out there. That's when I decided to set up on my own." If Texas had an asset to offer Hall and Sharp it was a burgeoning aerospace industry in the wake of America's commitment to go to the moon. While envisioning a mid-engined car with many of the characteristics of an American-engined Lotus 19—and using mostly Lotus suspension—Hall wanted the latest in frame technology. He found it at PlasTrend of Fort Worth, where Andy Green was prepared to make a complete monocoque frame of glass-reinforced epoxy plastic. Four such frames were made, three of which became cars.

The first Chaparral 2 made its bow at Riverside late in 1963. It was a stunning debut for Hall with pole position, the first lap of that track at more than 100 mph and an early lead before retirement with an electrical fire. While Jim's car was Chevrolet-powered with a Colotti gearbox, Hap preferred the smaller Oldsmobile engine with a Cooper box. "With 25 starts in 15 events," said Hall of 1964, "we recorded seven overall wins, six seconds, and two thirds. We attained the fastest lap at ten different major race tracks." Chaparral was on the map, big time.

Eager to keep up with the latest industry events, especially if they were GM-related, GM's Styling Staff made contact with the Chaparral principals and invited them to the GM Technical Center at Warren, Michigan. There they gained the enthusiastic support of racing-minded GM vice president Bill Mitchell, who asked his aerodynamicists and stylists to lend a hand. GM had just built the stunning Corvair Monza GT (see Ludvigsen Library Corvair book) which showed that the groups shared common ground. "In those days," Hall said later, "Bill Mitchell and Styling were about the only people interested in us."

While Styling's shapes influenced the look of the Chaparral 2, Chevrolet's hugely creative R&D department under Frank Winchell saw Chaparral Cars and its on-site test track as an ideal partner for its exploration of new engineering concepts for high-performance cars. Chevrolet made some mid-engined cars of its own, one of which used a simple torque converter as a transmission. With a Chevy V-8 tailored to it, this power train was plunked into a Chaparral 2 as an experiment for a race at Laguna Seca in May 1964. With Hall at the wheel it was a runaway winner. Henceforth all road-racing Chaparrals would use variations of this Chevrolet-built automatic. In August 1964 a two-speed version was racing and for 1966 a third speed was added.

Chaparral's successful 1965 season (16 wins in 21 races) started with its greatest triumph to date, victory in the Sebring 12-hour race against international competition. This encouraged Hall and Sharp to plan an international campaign for 1966. They rebodied two open Chaparral 2s to create the 2D coupe, designed to meet international regulations. One driven by Jo Bonnier and Phil Hill achieved a stunning success in the Nürburgring 1,000 kilometers. Rebuilt again as the winged Chaparral 2F for 1967, this model set the fastest lap in five of its eight entries and won the last race of its career at Brands Hatch in July 1967 in the hands of Mike Spence and Phil Hill. It was the latter's final race.

In 1966, Phil Hill introduced the winged Chaparral 2E to the Can-Am series in September at Bridgehampton, New York. Two such cars were made, using new lighter aluminum monocoques of a type that was first raced in the short-lived 2C at the end of 1965. These sensational-looking racers were fast but fragile, their best Can-Am result a one-two for Hill-Hall at Laguna Seca. One 2E was transformed into a 2G for the 1967 Can-Am, powered by a 7-liter aluminum V-8 built by Chevrolet. Also raced in 1968, this was not a happy car for Hall. It brought him no wins, three seconds, and a nine-week hospital stay plus six months in a wheelchair after a violent crash in the final 1968 race at Las Vegas.

In 1968's Can-Am series Jim should have been driving his latest creation, the 2H, but severe development problems delayed its launch to 1969. This was an ultra-radical super-low racer with a complex glass-fiber monocoque harking back to Chaparral's structural origins. Semi-invalid Hall engaged Briton John Surtees as the team's driver, but the two didn't get on well. Further delays with the 2H saw a Chaparral-entered McLaren M12 in five races and the 2H in five others. In practice for the sixth and last 1969 race the 2H was damaged beyond immediate repair.

Jim Hall stepped back into the cockpit in 1970 when Chaparral Cars fielded a team of Camaros in the Can-Am for Chevrolet. The team scored one win with Vic Elford at the wheel. Known to the team as "Quick Vic," Briton Elford was also the driver for three of the four entries of the most controversial Can-Am car of all time, the Chaparral 2J. This used a separate engine to drive two fans that exhausted air from beneath the car to create road-gripping suction downforce. Based on a Chevrolet-built prototype, the 2J was raced prematurely and banned quickly after sitting on the pole in three of its four starts.

One challenge remained for the competitive Hall: Indianapolis. He tested there with a sports car in 1964 and planned a winged 1967 entry but high wings were banned so he regrouped. From 1972 through 1975 he was a partner with Chicagoan Carl Haas in a Formula 5000 team that enjoyed great success with driver Brian Redman. They used a Lola, and when Chaparral thoughts turned again to Indy in 1978 Lola supplied a car to Hall's specification, which promptly won the 500-mile classic with Al Unser at the wheel.

For 1979 Jim Hall decided to build his own car and the last Chaparral, the 2K, was created. English designer John Barnard endowed it with the downforce-generating underbody tunnels just coming into Formula 1; Hall was again using the wind to help him. With Unser the 2K dominated from pole in 1979 before its transmission failed. In 1980, Johnny Rutherford won both the Indy 500 and the USAC championship with the 2K, one of the winningest Chaparrals.

In the twenty-first century six-foot-three Jim Hall enjoyed showing off his road-racing Chaparrals, beautifully restored by long-time team member Troy Rogers. But in their heyday Hall was anything but a show-off. His plain-white cars arrived at their races on trailers behind white pick-up trucks with camper bodies. In 1969, I wrote as follows about his still-secret 2H: "When it's ready it will race, and when it races it will speak for itself, with authority, doing what it does well, making no excuses, arriving and leaving without fanfare, running the fast and fair way. Just like the man who built it." I can't improve on that as a description of the man and his cars.

To the tune of $16,500, Texan Jim Hall backed the plan of Dick Troutman and Tom Barnes to produce a series of front-engine sports-racing cars. Their mutual aim was to make the car a commercial proposition. Hall tested the first prototype Chaparral, still unpainted, at Riverside in June 1961.

Powered by the ubiquitous Chevrolet V-8 at 283 cubic inches, the prototype Chaparral had an aluminum body styled by industrial designer Chuck Pelly. Its tubular-steel space frame carried independent suspension at all four wheels. This first car had an 88-inch wheelbase but later Chaparrals were lengthened to 90 inches.

A feature of the first Chaparral was its positioning of fuel tanks to the left and right of the cockpit. Although this helped keep the weight of the fuel within the wheelbase, it meant that the Chaparral had insufficient weight on its rear wheels for optimum traction during much of a race. Its instrument panel was exiguous.

Tom Barnes, left, and Dick Troutman checked the condition of their first Chaparral during its maiden test in June 1961. Driver/owner/backer Jim Hall sat thoughtfully behind its wheel. The Chevrolet engine's initial complement of three Stromberg carburetors was later doubled to six.

One of the great stars of American road racing in the 1960s, Jim Hall, left, was the complete competitor, marrying the activities of executive, team manager, designer, engineer, test driver, and racing driver. For Hall speed and innovation counted; winning championships was secondary. His ally in Chaparral Cars was Hap Sharp, right. A more complex character, Sharp was an important source of ideas and a very quick driver. Hap would often enjoy successes when Jim's car retired after the failure of some experimental part he was testing.

At the age of 28, Jim Hall sat in the cockpit of his first Chaparral 2 in the Bahamas for Nassau Speed Week in December 1963. The dark area below the belt line represented the all-glass-fiber monocoque produced for Hall by Andy Green. Wheels were of Lotus pattern but specially cast by the Texans with additional stiffening ribs.

Jim Hall was pictured by Stanley Rosenthall passing the pits on his way to victory at Watkins Glen in a race for the US Road Racing Championship (USRRC) on June 28, 1964. This was the third race in which the GM torque-converter transmission was used. An extra oil cooler for the transmission was piped from the aperture in the rear transom to a position above the rear spoiler.

A front view of the Chaparral 2 at Watkins Glen showed its transmission oil cooler attached to the rear spoiler. The scoop in the "passenger door" fed air to an engine oil cooler. The superiority of the Chaparral 2 at the Glen was such that Hall lapped all other competitors save his teammate Roger Penske.

As seen at Watkins Glen in June 1964 the Chaparral 2 had a purposeful look at the rear, a view seen by all its competitors. The squared-off rear, fitted with Corvair tail lamps, was aerodynamically efficient. The exhaust pipes, trailing back through gaps in the rear spoiler, were new that June for the 327-cubic-inch Chevrolet engine.

At Watkins Glen in June 1964 Roger Penske drove the sister Chaparral 2 with its Colotti gearbox. The engines used by Chaparral had aluminum blocks, which Penske had been instrumental in creating when he was working for Alcoa. At the Glen he stalled his car at the start but came back through the field to finish second behind the boss.

In the cockpit of the Chaparral 2 the driver sat directly on the surface of the glass-fiber and epoxy monocoque. Fuel tanks in the side sponsons were joined to a third central tank beneath the driver's knees. With no shift positions save reverse, neutral, and go, the small lever at the driver's right was a rudimentary affair.

Chaparral Cars prepared thoroughly for Sebring's 12-hour race on March 27, 1965. Two 2s were readied and a 12-hour endurance test was successfully completed at Rattlesnake Raceway. In the extremely wet race one car was severely delayed but the other, driven by Hall and Sharp, vanquished all comers to win outright.

The subject of intense speculation among competitors and the press, the Chaparral 2 automatic transmission was always covered with a tarpaulin whenever the rear deck was open. In fact, as the photograph on the right indicates, there was very little to see. The geared element of the transmission was a simple two-shaft all-indirect gearbox with its speeds engaged by dog clutches on its input shaft. Shifts were clutchless with the driver simply backing off the throttle and shifting either up or down.

Shown in the experimental Chevrolet CERV II, the GM automatic transmission also used by Chaparral allowed the driver to brake with his left foot. The creation of Jerry Mrlik and Joe Kurleto of Chevrolet R&D, the transmission depended for its function on a specially designed torque converter in place of the clutch. In this respect it functioned exactly like the original Buick Dynaflow automatic transmission of 1948.

Looking little changed in May 1965 the extremely straightforward Chaparral 2 cockpit now had a cushion for the driver. A lock-out ring had to be lifted to engage reverse gear in the two-speed transaxle. The transmission's spur gears were small in diameter and fine-pitched. They were engaged by small-diameter dog clutches, each with three bold dogs, designed to stay engaged until the throttle was released.

Needing a more open design of wheel to provide better brake cooling, Chaparral asked for the thoughts of Chevrolet R&D. The result was the above design by Chevy's Frank Boehm. With pioneering split rims that allowed rim widths to be varied, the wheels were cast for Chaparral by Arlington Industries at Arlington, Texas. Engines were built for Chaparral by Art Oehrli in California. Extremely long inlet ram pipes and individual exhaust pipes gave the wide torque curve that worked best with the torque-converter automatic transmission—here covered with the usual tarpaulin.

Hall and Sharp originally planned to build the Chaparral 2 as a coupe, using a shape not unlike that of the Chevrolet Corvair Monza GT. Although an open configuration was chosen instead, some of that car's frontal aspect was still visible in the neat style of its nose and inset headlamps. Hap Sharp's car at Bridgehampton in May 1965 was fitted with small spoilers just forward of each front wheel.

The USRRC race at Bridgehampton, Long Island, on May 23, 1965 was for the Vanderbilt Cup as well, a famous American racing trophy first presented in 1904. Driving his customary number 66, Jim Hall won the race and was awarded the trophy by Cornelius Vanderbilt. As so often that year, both Chaparrals lapped the entire field.

In the Bridgehampton USRRC in May 1965 Hap Sharp started from pole and finished second. His rear-wheel openings had been cut away to provide clearance for larger Firestone tires. Working closely with Firestone, Hall took the sister car to Indianapolis in June, where he turned laps at 145 mph during that tire company's test sessions for Indy cars. Even wider rear tires were experimented with there.

After their abortive start with a high-nose configuration, the Chaparral crew was successful with a low chisel nose for their model 2, combined with a high tail topped by an adjustable spoiler. Hall initiated his serious study of racecar aerodynamics after he was dismayed to discover that his first mid-engined car went quicker at Rattlesnake Raceway without its body. "I've got all that force to deal with," Hall decided at the time. "Why don't I use it to help me?"

In the midst of the sand dunes around Bridgehampton near the tip of Long Island Hap Sharp and his wife drove their racecar to the circuit in May 1965. Stanley Rosenthall took this picture on race day, when the car's nose spoilers were already in position. Between them was the low scoop that admitted air to the car's radiator.

Maneuvering into the Bridgehampton paddock during practice, Hap Sharp helped push his Chaparral 2 while Troy Rogers took the wheel. Rogers often drove the Chaparrals during tests at Rattlesnake Raceway. The availability of a test track adjacent to the factory was an amenity not then enjoyed by any other racing-car builder and was only equaled later by Ferrari with its track at Fiorano.

Having established the merits of spoilers under the nose, Hall appeared at Canada's Mosport Park early in June 1965 with much-enhanced deflectors in front of the wheels. Hall and his team took particular care in preparing their car appropriately for each type of circuit. Mosport was notorious for its dips and rises that could send a car flying. Hall had in fact broken his left arm in a crash there the previous year—although not for that reason—and thus had been unable to race for the balance of the 1964 season.

An overhead view by Stanley Rosenthall displayed the Chaparral's remarkably uncluttered and functional lines. The driver was deeply enclosed by his Plexiglas windscreen with its neat veed shape. A central grille relieved air pressure in the front compartment and a vent released warm air from the front-mounted engine radiator.

Jim Hall and the Chaparral 2 set new benchmarks for speed in the Players 200 at Mosport Park on June 4, 1965. In practice Hall was the first to lap Mosport at better than 100 mph, taking pole position, and he also set a lap record at 101.52 mph.

At Mosport in June 1965 Hall won the first 100-mile heat from John Surtees and Bruce McLaren. Pit stops with throttle problems delayed him in the second heat. Hall finished seventh and was classified second overall.

The ability of the split-rim Chaparral wheel to be expanded to make use of wider tires was well demonstrated by Jim Hall's car at St. Jovite on Independence Day of 1965. A tire war between Firestone and Goodyear caused the steady widening of the Chaparral's rear bodywork. A fold-down door met the letter of the SCCA's rules.

So neat and well detailed was the bodywork of the Chaparral 2 that its fuel fillers were even concealed under hinged lids. Here Jim Hall's car was given a top-up. The scrutineers at St. Jovite required its headlamps to be taped.

During the 1965 season the Chaparrals acquired air scoops placed low at the rear of their monocoques to provide air to the rear brakes. Additional cooling was required, both because no engine braking was possible or even desirable with the automatic transmission, and because the rear brakes were becoming more deeply shrouded by the wider Firestone tires and their wheels.

At Canada's St. Jovite on July 4, 1965, Jim Hall battled bravely with Bruce McLaren's M1A but had to admit defeat. Jim set the fastest lap on his way to second place while Hap Sharp finished third. The next six races brought six wins in a row, divided equally between Hall and Sharp.

Racing successfully in 1965 with his automatic transmission, Hall kept the long inlet ram pipes that bolstered the lower regions of his engine's torque curve. They were mounted above 48-mm Weber twin-throat carburetors. The Chevy V-8 engine developed on the order of 450 horsepower.

Visible in the cockpit of the Chaparral 2 were the vertical louvers which vented air pressure from its front wheelhouses to reduce front-end lift. During practice the passenger's seat was often occupied by a data-gathering tape recorder which downloaded information on circuit speed and other conditions. Both Chaparral and Chevrolet used the data for analysis and race preparation.

As raced so successfully at Sebring in March 1965 the Chaparral 2 cockpit looked little different than it did for its sprint-racing appearances. The flap over the fuel filler had to be fitted with a special latch so that it could be sealed after refueling by the Sebring pit marshals.

The driver of the Chaparral 2 couldn't ask for a simpler instrument panel. The Chevrolet engine was most effective between 5,000 and 7,200 rpm, as monitored by the small-diameter electronic tachometer. Fuses were readily accessible; in a race at Continental Divide in Colorado during August 1965 Jim Hall had to replace a blown fuel-pump fuse to finish fourth while Hap Sharp won.

Hap Sharp favored goggles for his drive at St. Jovite's Mont Tremblant circuit in July 1965. The gearing of the Chaparrals for each circuit was organized so as to require the minimum amount of shifting for each lap, allowing the torque converter's range to cover as much of the road-speed variation as possible.

The successes of Hap Sharp (here at St. Jovite) during 1965 were gratifying for Chaparral but unhelpful for Jim Hall, who was trying to repeat his 1964 USRRC Championship. In the end Hall was best of the big-car drivers but was pipped to the official crown by George Follmer in a parallel championship for 2-liter cars.

By September 1965 the Chaparral crew had heavily louvered the front fenders of their racecar. They concluded that the more louvers the better, although they were very difficult to execute in glass-fiber. A special duct was also added to deliver fresh air to the driver, here a happy Hap Sharp at Bridgehampton.

Against serious international opposition Hap Sharp was the winner of the Bridgehampton Double 500 held over 310 miles on the two days of September 18 and 19, 1965. This was a fine victory for the mercurial and determined Sharp, who brought great vigor and attack to the Chaparral effort.

As part of its experimentation with high-performance vehicles Frank Winchell's Chevrolet R&D department built the GSIIb, using a bonded and riveted aluminum monocoque designed under the direction of engineer Jim Musser. At 70 pounds the monocoque weighed half as much as the fiberglass tub hitherto used by Chaparral.

The Chevrolet GSIIb, shown, was never raced. However, Chevrolet gave it to Chaparral, where its monocoque inspired that of the Chaparral 2C that raced at the end of 1965. Its design featured a low sill level because consideration was being given to building a coupe version of the GSIIb. (See Ludvigsen Library book on Corvette exotic prototypes.)

While the open-cockpit Chaparrals made a transition to aluminum monocoques, the thrifty Midlanders built endurance-racing coupes on their original glass-fiber tubs. Thus was born the Chaparral 2D, creating at last the enclosed coupe that had been considered at the beginning of the program.

A single Chaparral 2D was ready in time for the Daytona 24 Hours raced on February 5 and 6, 1966. Driven by Phil Hill and Jo Bonnier, it qualified second fastest against strong opposition from the latest Fords and Ferraris.

Co-driver Jo Bonnier, left, joined Troy Rogers next to the Chaparral 2D before the start of the 1966 race at Daytona. Within the contours of the original Chaparral 2 nose a substantial battery of headlamps had been incorporated. As prepared for endurance racing, its 327-cubic-inch Chevrolet V-8 was rated at 420 bhp at 6,800 rpm.

Changes to the nose of the 2D for Sebring in March 1966 included air inlets for cockpit ventilation and a transverse spoiler to encourage air to exit the radiator. Two cars were entered but both retired after experiencing serious engine problems in practice that were later traced to piston rings that failed to seat.

Although it showed impressive speed in practice at Daytona in February 1966, the Chaparral 2D was still early in its development. During practice a need for additional engine oil cooling was identified and an external cooler (not shown here) was added adjacent to the right-hand rear window.

With Phil Hill at its wheel the new 2D underwent inspection during a night practice session in preparation for the 1966 Daytona 24-Hour race. Owing to the heavy downforce produced by Daytona's high banking it was essential to check for proper clearance of its tires against the bodywork, as a team member was doing here.

The 2D had a rear spoiler under the driver's control. With his left foot having nothing to do but apply the brake, the driver pressed a third pedal on the straightaway to feather the rear spoiler, thus increasing the car's speed potential. When he released the pedal to apply the brakes the spoiler defaulted to its full-downforce position.

The moveable rear Chaparral 2D spoiler was in its high-downforce position as the car sat in the pits at Daytona. After Phil Hill got into a twist with his adjustable spoiler during the race and retired with a broken suspension upright, Jim Hall decided that it was a complication he could do without. Hall rebuilt the 2D with an enclosed rear roof line and a conventional tail spoiler for Sebring and subsequent races.

After the problems experienced at Daytona and Sebring, Rattlesnake Raceway saw extensive testing of the 2D in preparation for a trip to Europe to race at the Nürburgring (shown) and Le Mans. The conventional rear spoiler adopted for Sebring was retained and a roof-top scoop was added to feed air to the carburetors.

The lone 2D sent to Europe had a new rear body panel with built-in air scoops and a revised nose to raise its headlamps and provide two small air inlets for cockpit cooling. Max Le Grand photographed it here on the Nürburgring's Karussell.

The result was spectacularly better at the historic Nürburgring, where the white coupe with the Texas license plate scored a sensational victory. Hill and Bonnier were the victors in front of a crowd that found it hard to take in the fact that a car with an automatic transmission had won over 1,000 kilometers (more than 600 miles) of the Nürburgring, the world's most demanding road course.

Hap Sharp, in dark shirt, was team manager for the European Chaparral racing effort in 1966. He was talking with helmeted Joe Bonnier and Phil Hill at Le Mans in June, where the 2D failed to feature and retired after ten hours.

If their European campaign with the 2D lacked the full attention of the small Chaparral crew at Midland it was because they were preparing this staggeringly revolutionary automobile for the 1966 Can-Am series. This rich new racing series, exceptionally well sponsored and promoted, rewarded and inspired the best efforts of teams, engineers, and drivers on both sides of the Atlantic.

Jim Hall's search for a clear understanding of the application of aerodynamics to a road-racing car reached its apotheosis in the 1966 Chaparral 2E. Its high rear-mounted wing applied downforce directly to its rear-wheel hubs, bypassing the sprung chassis. With its engine-cooling radiators moved to the rear, the nose duct of the 2E was available solely to add balancing downforce for its front wheels.

The rear wing was a joint inspiration of Jim Hall and Chevrolet engineers Jerry Mrlik, Jim Musser, and Frank Winchell, as U.S. patent 3,455,594 for it testifies. The wing itself was an ultra-light monocoque of thin glass-fiber skin filled with foam, made at Chevrolet by Joe Kurleto. Chaparral built its mountings and control system.

Built on the aluminum monocoque first used at the end of 1965 for the 2C, the 2E had a more cramped cockpit than the 2, requiring a removable steering wheel for entry. Networks of holes instead of the more time-consuming louvers released air pressure from the front wheelhouses. In both design and detail finish the shape and fabrication of the 2E was a tribute to the skills of the engineers and technicians at Midland.

Compared to the Lola T70 seen behind it at its Bridgehampton debut in September 1966, the 2E looked light-years in advance. Yet a Lola-Chevrolet was the Can-Am champion in 1966, with 2E drivers Phil Hill and Jim Hall fourth and fifth in the points respectively. Reliability was a problem, with three failures to finish from nine starts.

Air from the two engine-cooling radiators at the rear of the 2E was exhausted upward, adding to the car's downforce generation. Under its handsome rear deck was a 327-cubic-inch Chevrolet V-8 rated at 450 bhp at 6,800 rpm, driving through Chevrolet's two-speed torque-converter transmission. In the 1966 Can-Am races the cars gained one victory and three second places.

Any discussion of which of the fabulous Chaparrals is the most fabulous must include the 1967 2F. Understandably a crowd surrounded the 2F from Texas as it awaited the start of the Targa Florio in Sicily on May 14. A wheel chock rested on the grille above its engine bay. Bravely Hap Sharp joined Phil Hill for the demanding Targa but a deflated rear tire put them out of the running.

Returning to the Nürburgring for the 1,000 kilometers on May 28, Chaparral hoped for a repeat victory with the 2F. Phil Hill and Mike Spence were doing well—as shown here by Edward Eves—but were forced out by a failure of their three-speed General Motors transaxle.

Like the 2E, the 2F had its water radiators mounted in its hips. Behind them were smaller radiators for oil cooling, one for the transaxle and the other for the engine. By 1967 Chaparral was no longer using split wheel rims. The 16-inch spoked wheels of the 2F were cast in one piece at Arlington, Texas.

An aluminum box attached to the front of the glass-fiber tub of the Chaparral 2F carried many essential components. An oval opening housed its horns and carried cooling air to the cockpit. Brake-cooling air flowed through a rectangular opening, next to which was a spring-loaded panel, which opened above 120 mph to provide an aerodynamic stabilizing effect. Above it was an additional engine oil cooler added during the 1967 season to cope with the requirements of the 427-cubic-inch V-8.

Two of the magnificent 2F Chaparrals were prepared for Le Mans in June 1967. Chaparral crewmembers recalled that the two were absolutely identical. Narrow slots above the inlets to the two hip radiators provided air to the carburetors, which were Chevrolet-made replicas of 58-mm Webers. A new feature introduced by Chaparral was a slim aerodynamic splitter just below the front air intake.

Mounted directly to its rear hubs, the struts holding the 2F's wing were located by longitudinal radius rods and a transverse Watts linkage pivoted on a vertical aluminum triangle, an upward extension from the frame. At the rear of the chassis an aluminum box carried the exhaust-pipe outlets and the taillights, which were taken from a Chevrolet pick-up truck.

The three-speed transaxle used by Chaparral in 1967 was revealed to the camera of Edward Eves when the team decided to make a repair to an oil seal during the 24 Hours of Le Mans. To the left and right of it are oil reservoirs while the Watts linkage locating the wing's struts was visible at the top.

With the transaxle removed the 427-cubic-inch V-8 engine supplied by Chevrolet was visible. As used in endurance races it produced between 475 and 525 bhp at 6,000 rpm. Its high torque placed a heavy load on the transaxle, which overheated in the tight confines of the 2F's enclosed engine bay.

One Chaparral 2F was prepared for Phil Hill and Mike Spence to drive at Brands Hatch in the final international endurance race of the season over 1,000 kilometers on July 30, 1967. Finally the team had learned enough about the transaxle to give it the reliability needed to survive the race. On the twisty Brands circuit the wing was here in high-downforce position; the driver could feather it with his left foot.

Like the other runners at Brands Hatch, the 2F carried the Speedbird motif of race sponsor BOAC. Hill and Spence fought off tough competition from Lola, Ferrari, Mirage, and Porsche, and made up time after a pit stop for a puncture to achieve a tremendously popular victory for the white coupe from Texas.

Benefiting from the aerodynamic research conducted for the 2F, the 1966 2E Chaparral was transformed into the 2G for the 1967 Can-Am season. To add front downforce it was given air deflectors blended into its lower front fender lines. The "lower lip" between the two inlets for brake-cooling air was an aerodynamic deflector used only in the early part of the season.

The 2G was distinguished from the 2E by its much flatter flanks and its ducting to and from the side-mounted radiators like that of the 2F. Compare with photographs on pages 58 and 59. The Cox decal symbolized an arrangement under which Chaparral Cars earned royalties from the sale of Cox's models of its automobiles. This provided useful additional funding for the small company.

Still using the low-sided aluminum monocoque introduced at the end of 1965, the 2G had a deeply upholstered seat to help its driver cope with the higher lateral cornering forces generated by both increased downforce and steady Firestone tire improvements. A gate was now needed for the shift lever because the 2G used Chevrolet's three-speed-plus-converter transaxle.

The rear view of the 2G was simplicity itself. The two exhaust pipes exited at the center, above the single tail lamp replacing the two fitted to the 2E. Because one of Chaparral's aluminum chassis had been crashed beyond repair at Nassau the previous December by Hap Sharp, only a single 2G was prepared for the 1967 Can-Am season. Jim Hall was its driver.

Chevrolet supplied its all-aluminum 427-cubic-inch V-8 to Chaparral for the 2G, competing during the 1967 season with fuel injection. The use of this engine was premature, in Hall's judgement, but Chevrolet was eager to see it employed so he acquiesced. In both its supporting struts and its size the 2G's rear wing was substantially increased over that used in 1966.

Jim Hall stood by as his team buttoned up the 2G in the pits at Bridgehampton on September 17, 1967. At the higher power levels needed to be competitive in the Can-Am series Chevrolet's V-8 proved troublesome; Hall suffered 11 engine failures in six race entries. His best finishes were second at Laguna Seca and Riverside, and fourth at Elkhart Lake where he set fastest lap.

In 1968's Can-Am season Jim Hall planned to race his radical new 2H, but at the last minute it was declared unfit to compete. Jim hauled out his 1967 2G and updated it with wider wheels and tires. Here at Edmonton, Canada, on September 29 he suffered from grabbing rear brakes and made a lengthy pit stop, finishing 11th.

Hall's modified 2G first appeared at Elkhart Lake, Wisconsin. A prominent new feature was a forward-facing scoop to deliver ram air to the engine's intakes. In a rainy race at Elkhart's Road America Hall finished fifth.

As in the 2F the vertical struts supporting the 2G's wing were located laterally by a Watts linkage, mounted on an A-frame extension, but the pivot axis of the central link was vertical instead of horizontal. Oil reservoirs for both engine and transmission were located at the extreme rear of the chassis, flanking the transaxle.

Positioned high in the chassis, the 2G's exhaust manifold closely flanked the cylinder heads and curved around the wing struts to large collectors at the rear of the chassis. Between them was the ignition system and the fuel injection for the big Chevrolet V-8.

Supplied to Hall by Chevrolet, the 427-cubic-inch V-8 had aluminum cylinder block and heads with magnesium finned rocker covers and sump. Fitted here were narrow Firestones which the Chaparral crew converted into rain tires by carving away two circumferential areas of the tread.

Although similar to the engine used in 1967, the 1968 V-8 for the 2G had much longer inlet ram pipes to provide better medium-speed torque. Fuel vaporization was improved by placing the fuel-injection nozzles high in the side of each ram pipe. As first established with the 2E, the radiator header tank rested behind the driver's head.

The crude-looking pickup-style rear fender extensions, hastily added by Chaparral to accommodate wider tires for the 1968 2G, look empty at Elkhart Lake where the narrower rain tires were used. Hall placed fifth there behind the British McLarens, headed by the orange factory cars.

Here being chased through Echo Valley by two McLarens at Bridgehampton on September 15, Jim Hall was a contender for the lead on this demanding Long Island, New York, circuit. A clogged injector delayed him and he finished second to Mark Donohue, third in this photograph by Stanley Rosenthall.

Two trailing radius rods controlled each rear hub of the Chaparral 2G. The rods were angled to provide an anti-squat effect under acceleration. At the right was the aircraft-type battery that Hall preferred for his racing cars for its lightness and efficiency, although it turned out to be underpowered for his endurance racers.

In the nose of the 2G was a flap valve in an upward-flowing duct. It is seen here in its open position, when the duct generated maximum downforce. When the driver pressed a left-hand pedal on the straights, the valve closed the duct and reduced both drag and downforce at the front of the Chaparral 2G.

Jim Hall's 1968 Can-Am season brought him little satisfaction and ended with a serious crash at Las Vegas. In five starts his best finishes were second at Bridgehampton and third, here, at Riverside on October 27. He started among the leading McLarens of Denny Hulme and Mark Donohue.

At Riverside Jim Hall was delayed by a pit stop to rectify brake problems. As the pit signs indicate, however, Hall was nevertheless a strong competitor, but in the end he had to settle for third place. In its next race, at Las Vegas, the 2G was destroyed and Jim Hall seriously injured.

For his 1968 Can-Am season Jim Hall conceived a completely new Chaparral, the 2H, designed and built in Midland. Although originally built as an enclosed coupe, at the request of contracted driver John Surtees it was modified before it raced to give the driver a more exposed position. A bemused crowd inspected the 2H at Edmonton, Canada, where Surtees drove it to sixth in its delayed 1969 debut.

Added to the 2H during its protracted development were additional fenced downforce-generating winglets athwart its nose. The 2H represented the ultimate in a monocoque construction using resin reinforced by glass-fiber, its entire shell serving as a structural element of the vehicle. Only the rear deck, lifted here, was not structural.

The 2H concept was to combine 20-inch-wide rear Firestone tires with an extremely low-drag vehicle to achieve optimum lap times. That Jim Hall embraced this concept was baffling to his friends at Chevrolet, who believed that their mutual test results had demonstrated the benefit of downforce above all as a generator of fast lap times.

Visible in the foreground is the articulated de Dion axle that connected the rear wheels of the 2H. Its problems had been crucial in the one-year delay of its debut. In its five appearances in the 1969 Can-Am season the exotic 2H failed to finish three times and achieved a best placing of fifth at Mid-Ohio, with John Surtees at the wheel.

Although it made its debut a year late, the Chaparral 2H was still not ready for the start of the 1969 Can-Am season. To fill the gap Chaparral Cars acquired a McLaren M12 and modified it to use a Chaparral wing and an engine similar to that of the 2H. John Surtees drove it four times, finishing third in the season opener at Mosport on June 1.

An unwell John Surtees recommended Italian Andrea de Adamich to deputize for him in the Chaparral McLaren M12 at Michigan International Raceway on September 28, 1969. De Adamich made good use of the car in his one and only drive for the Chaparral team, finishing fifth.

As prepared by Chaparral for the 1969 Can-Am wars, the McLaren M12 had the same special horizontal inlet manifold of magnesium that had been designed for the 2H. A vertically mounted Vertex magneto supplied its sparks and fuel injection was by a Lucas system modified by Chaparral. A special tower at the rear of the frame carried the Watts linkage locating the struts holding the rear wing.

The McLaren M12 entered by Chaparral as a substitute for the 2H during 1969 was a production car built by Trojan to McLaren designs. The radius rods guiding the struts that held its big rear wing were pivoted from its rollover bar. The car's first winged appearance was in its third race for Chaparral, here at Watkins Glen on July 13. Problems with overheating relegated Surtees to a 12th-place finish.

In mid-1970, Jim Hall looked at the birdie from the cockpit of his latest creation, the Chaparral 2J. The result of a combined effort between Chaparral Cars and Chevrolet R&D, the 2J was the innovative elixir that Hall needed after his troubled Can-Am seasons of 1968 and 1969. Looking, as one commentator said, "like the box it came in," the 2J introduced suction ground effects to automobile racing.

Shown, as at left, at Midland's Rattlesnake Raceway prior to its racing debut, the 2J was sucked against the road surface by two extractor fans mounted at its extreme rear. Hall's 2J was a much-improved (by Chaparral) evolution of a crude test vehicle built by Chevrolet R&D to explore this radical concept.

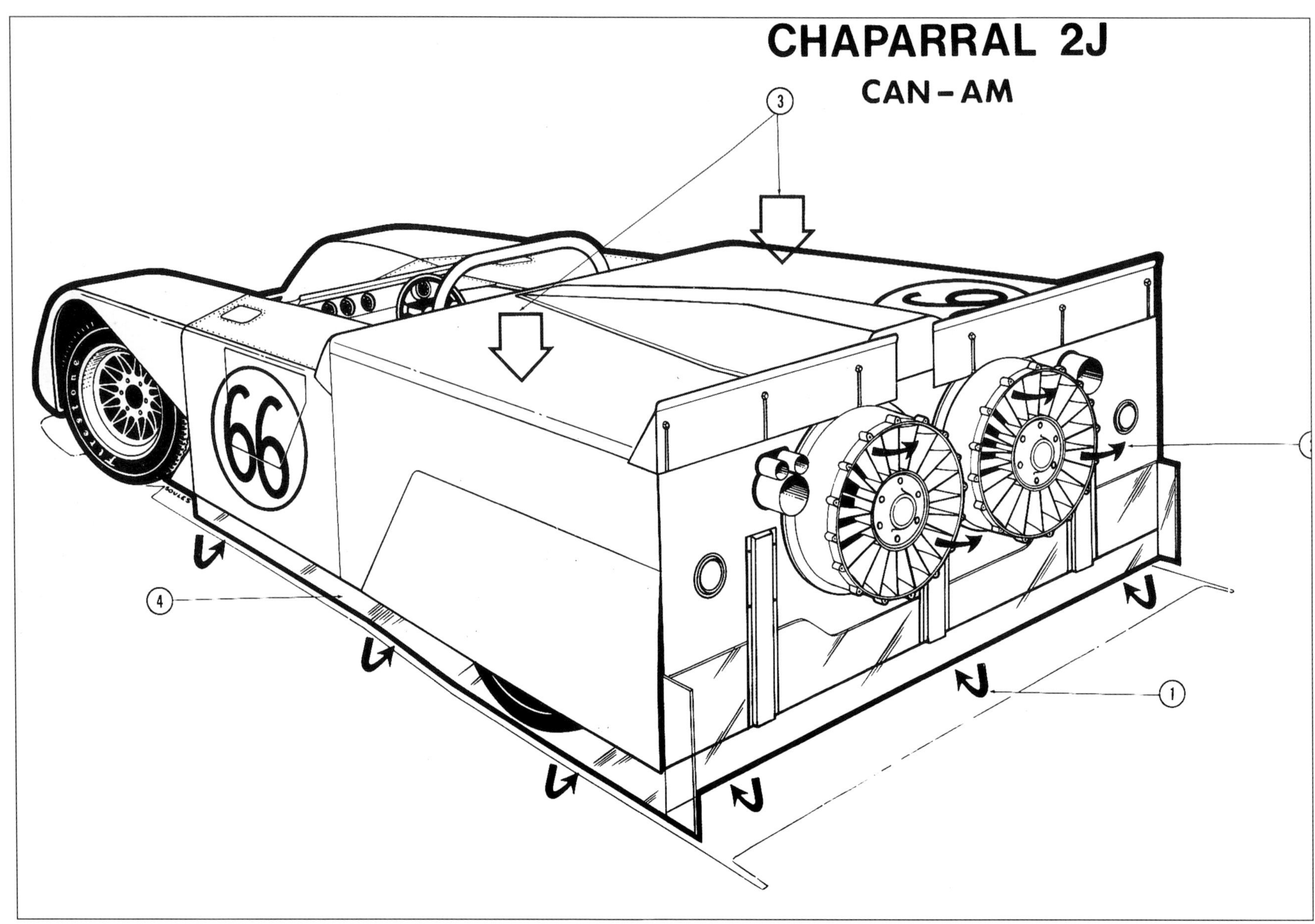

A diagram explained the concept of the Chaparral 2J. Driven at a constant speed of some 5,000 rpm by a separate engine, the twin 17-inch fans at the rear extracted air from an enclosed area of the 2J extending from the rear of the front wheels all the way to the extreme tail. At the side and rear, skirts made of tough GE Lexan plastic ensured that the suction was highly effective by staying close to the road surface.

The central section of the Chaparral 2J was a deep and rugged aluminum monocoque tub. It used front suspension similar to that of the 2H and rear suspension adapted from the 2G. That the suspension geometries provided anti-dive and anti-squat was particularly useful for the 2J, which needed to ride as flat and level as possible to maintain its ground-effect skirts in close proximity to the road.

The front end of the 2J Chaparral was shaped to divert as much air as possible up over the top of the vehicle and around its sides. Front air inlets were for the engine-cooling radiator and ducts to the front brakes. Slotted inlets on both sides of the rollover bar ingested induction air for the engine.

Defying convention in every respect, the spectacular Chaparral 2J made its debut at the Watkins Glen Can-Am race on July 12, 1970. Jim Hall felt that the entry was premature in view of the car's relatively untested status, but he wanted to race it before others got wind of its innovative attributes. After successfully completing a 200-mile test at Midland, the 2J was shaken down during the Tuesday and Wednesday before the Glen Can-Am.

Jim Hall obtained the services of reigning World Champion driver Jackie Stewart as his 2J pilot for the Watkins Glen Can-Am race. Hall was extremely satisfied with the services provided by Stewart, who extracted all of the car's considerable performance. In spite of a number of problems during practice Stewart qualified it in third place behind the factory-team McLarens of Dan Gurney and Denny Hulme.

In the Can-Am race at the Glen Jackie Stewart set the fastest lap with the 2J before retiring with a variety of ailments, including brake problems, failure of its two-stroke fan-drive engine, and a missed shift. Nevertheless the radical car had shown its pace.

Ducts from the air inlets athwart the cockpit provided fresh ram air to the inlet manifold of the 2J, carried over from the 2H. In the foreground, attached to the rear suspension by a Bowden cable, was the bell-crank linkage that kept the Lexan side skirt close to the ground as the rear of the Chaparral rose and fell over bumps.

Originally the cogged-rubber drive belts from the auxiliary engine to the two extractor fans were located inboard of the fans. This arrangement proved vulnerable to debris sucked up from the road, which dislodged the drive belts. During the season the belts were relocated outboard of the fans and enclosed by an exotic cover nicknamed by one crewmember the "Martian bra." The 2J's engine exhaust emerged on both sides of its fans.

The Chaparral 2H carried over Chevrolet's torque-converter transmission with a three-gear dog-clutch box. Perched atop this was the engine that drove the extractor fans, a two-cylinder two-stroke air-cooled JLO engine usually found in snowmobiles. Disc brakes were internally ventilated.

Chaparral engine man Gary Knutson equipped the JLO engine with fuel injection and capacitive-discharge ignition to enhance its reliability. Nevertheless it showed a tendency to run well at Midland but to give trouble when the 2H visited the Can-Am tracks. With the engine running at full throttle all the time, the 2J driver had to monitor its cylinder-head temperature and adjust its mixture. He was often too busy to carry out this task.

Stripped of its front and rear body sections, the 2J revealed its deep central aluminum monocoque structure. Its hinged "doors" met the letter of the Can-Am regulations. Standing behind the car in sunglasses was Cameron Argetsinger, spark plug of road racing at Watkins Glen, who had joined Chaparral Cars as a vice president in 1970.

Providing the vital seal at the front of the suction area under the Chaparral 2J was a transverse row of a dozen Lexan plaques. Each of the plaques comprised an individual system, with a plastic hinge to the body. As designed by Chevrolet's Don Gates, each was backed up by two more Lexan plaques, which were hinged to it in such a way as to harness both spring and vacuum force to keep its trailing edge firmly against the pavement.

Next to a Porsche 917, considered one of the most advanced conventional racers of 1970, the Chaparral 2J was a startling sight. Measurements conducted by Chaparral showed it to be capable of cornering at least seven percent faster than the dominant Can-Am McLarens.

As much for its potential as for its performance, the Chaparral 2J caused great consternation in the Can-Am ranks. Rivals had recourse to the rule books, which stated that moving parts with an aerodynamic function were banned. In 1970, this regulation had caused the elimination of high movable wings. It was concluded that both the rotating fans and the movable skirt contravened this regulation. At the end of the season both would be banned.

Among the gauges facing the driver of the 2J was one which told him how much suction was being generated. Tests showed that when suction was lost the Chaparral remained easily controllable. He was also informed about the cylinder-head temperature of the auxiliary engine. The steering wheel was quick-removable for easy entry.

Briton Vic Elford drove the 2J in the three more Can-Am races it contested after Watkins Glen. Elford was on pole in all three races. At Road Atlanta the auxiliary engine's problems demoted him to sixth. A Chevrolet engine failure kept him from starting at Laguna Seca, and at Riverside the auxiliary engine broke its crankshaft.

The Chaparral crew gave Jackie Stewart a push out of the pits in the 2J at Watkins Glen. After several troubled years Chaparral was again in the limelight, and with good reason. Although powered ground effects were banned, the same principle underpinned the use of venturi-generated ground effects toward the end of the 1970s.

Jim Hall leaned across Vic Elford into the cockpit of the 2J at Riverside in the radical car's last race appearance. Keeping the lap chart, Sandy Hall was protecting her eardrums. Although unsuccessful as a racing car, the 2J made history as the first car capable of generating so much downforce that it could be driven on the ceiling.

Resources that would have helped the preparation of the Chaparral 2J for the 1970 Can-Am season were otherwise committed to two Chevrolet Camaros for the SCCA's Trans-Am series. In 1970, this was at the height of its popularity, with entries from Ford, Plymouth, Dodge, Pontiac, and American Motors as well as Chevrolet.

As raced in 1969 by the Roger Penske team, the Camaro had been the Trans-Am champion. When Penske defected to American Motors to race its Javelin, Chevrolet asked Jim Hall to step in and prepare its handsome new Camaro.

Sanitary preparation by Chaparral Cars was evident under the hood of the 1970 Trans-Am Camaro. As the rules newly required, a single four-barrel carburetor sat atop its 302-cubic-inch V-8. The car's development problems during the season placed heavy demands on Chaparral's engineering capability.

Surrounded by a tubular steel roll cage, the Chaparral Camaro interior was ultra-professional. Among the drivers engaged for the team in 1970 were Ed Leslie, Milt Minter, Vic Elford, and Jim Hall himself. Elford brought the team its sole victory at Watkins Glen, New York.

The year 1970 was the last for the Chaparral sports cars. Hall turned instead to Indy-car racing, for which he decided to build a car of his own. The Chaparral 2K introduced in 1979 was designed by John Barnard and built in Britain by BS Fabrications. In a bow to sponsor Pennzoil, whose corporate color was yellow, it was the first non-white Chaparral.

Jim Hall shook the hand of Al Unser after he qualified the brand-new Chaparral 2K in the front row for the Indianapolis 500 in 1979. It won the last race of that season at Phoenix. Johnny Rutherford drove the Cosworth-powered 2K to an Indy victory and the CART championship in 1980. This, the final Chaparral, last raced in 1981.

MORE TITLES FROM ICONOGRAFIX:

AMERICAN CULTURE

AMERICAN SERVICE STATIONS 1935-1943 PHOTO ARCHIVE ISBN 1-882256-27-1
COCA-COLA: A HISTORY IN PHOTOGRAPHS 1930-1969 ISBN 1-882256-46-8
COCA-COLA: ITS VEHICLES IN PHOTOGRAPHS 1930-1969 ISBN 1-882256-47-6
PHILLIPS 66 1945-1954 PHOTO ARCHIVE ISBN 1-882256-42-5
RVs & CAMPERS 1900-2000: AN ILLUSTRATED HISTORY ISBN 1-58388-064-X

AUTOMOTIVE

AMX PHOTO ARCHIVE: FROM CONCEPT TO REALITY ISBN 1-58388-062-3
CADILLAC 1948-1964 PHOTO ALBUM ISBN 1-882256-83-2
CAMARO 1967-2000 PHOTO ARCHIVE ISBN 1-58388-032-1
CHEVROLET STATION WAGONS 1946-1966 PHOTO ARCHIVE ISBN 1-58388-069-0
CLASSIC AMERICAN LIMOUSINES 1955-2000 PHOTO ARCHIVE ISBN 1-58388-041-0
CORVAIR by CHEVROLET EXP. & PROD. CARS 1957-1969 LUDVIGSEN LIBRARY SERIES ISBN 1-58388-058-5
CORVETTE THE EXOTIC EXPERIMENTAL CARS, LUDVIGSEN LIBRARY SERIES ISBN 1-58388-017-8
CORVETTE PROTOTYPES & SHOW CARS PHOTO ALBUM ISBN 1-882256-77-8
EARLY FORD V-8S 1932-1942 PHOTO ALBUM ISBN 1-882256-97-2
IMPERIAL 1955-1963 PHOTO ARCHIVE ISBN 1-882256-22-0
IMPERIAL 1964-1968 PHOTO ARCHIVE ISBN 1-882256-23-9
LINCOLN MOTOR CARS 1920-1942 PHOTO ARCHIVE ISBN 1-882256-57-3
LINCOLN MOTOR CARS 1946-1960 PHOTO ARCHIVE ISBN 1-882256-58-1
PACKARD MOTOR CARS 1935-1942 PHOTO ARCHIVE ISBN 1-882256-44-1
PACKARD MOTOR CARS 1946-1958 PHOTO ARCHIVE ISBN 1-882256-45-X
PONTIAC DREAM CARS, SHOW CARS & PROTOTYPES 1928-1998 PHOTO ALBUM ISBN 1-882256-93-X
PONTIAC FIREBIRD TRANS-AM 1969-1999 PHOTO ALBUM ISBN 1-882256-95-6
PONTIAC FIREBIRD 1967-2000 PHOTO HISTORY ISBN 1-58388-028-3
STRETCH LIMOUSINES 1928-2001 PHOTO ARCHIVE ISBN 1-58388-070-4
STUDEBAKER 1933-1942 PHOTO ARCHIVE ISBN 1-882256-24-7
ULTIMATE CORVETTE TRIVIA CHALLENGE ISBN 1-58388-035-6

BUSES

BUSES OF MOTOR COACH INDUSTRIES 1932-2000 PHOTO ARCHIVE ISBN 1-58388-039-9
FLXIBLE TRANSIT BUSES 1953-1995 PHOTO ARCHIVE ISBN 1-58388-053-4
GREYHOUND BUSES 1914-2000 PHOTO ARCHIVE ISBN 1-58388-027-5
*MACK® BUSES 1900-1960 PHOTO ARCHIVE** ISBN 1-58388-020-8
TRAILWAYS BUSES 1936-2001 PHOTO ARCHIVE ISBN 1-58388-029-1
TROLLEY BUSES 1913-2001 PHOTO ARCHIVE ISBN 1-58388-057-7
YELLOW COACH BUSES 1923-1943 PHOTO ARCHIVE ISBN 1-58388-054-2

EMERGENCY VEHICLES

AMERICAN LAFRANCE 700 SERIES 1945-1952 PHOTO ARCHIVE ISBN 1-882256-90-5
AMERICAN LAFRANCE 700 SERIES 1945-1952 PHOTO ARCHIVE VOLUME 2 ISBN 1-58388-025-9
AMERICAN LAFRANCE 700 & 800 SERIES 1953-1958 PHOTO ARCHIVE ISBN 1-882256-91-3
AMERICAN LAFRANCE 900 SERIES 1958-1964 PHOTO ARCHIVE ISBN 1-58388-002-X
CROWN FIRECOACH 1951-1985 PHOTO ARCHIVE ISBN 1-58388-047-X
CLASSIC AMERICAN AMBULANCES 1900-1979 PHOTO ARCHIVE ISBN 1-882256-94-8
CLASSIC AMERICAN FUNERAL VEHICLES 1900-1980 PHOTO ARCHIVE ISBN 1-58388-016-X
CLASSIC SEAGRAVE 1935-1951 PHOTO ARCHIVE ISBN 1-58388-034-8
FIRE CHIEF CARS 1900-1997 PHOTO ALBUM ISBN 1-882256-87-5
HEAVY RESCUE TRUCKS 1931-2000 PHOTO GALLERY ISBN 1-58388-045-3
INDUSTRIAL AND PRIVATE FIRE APPARATUS 1925-2001 PHOTO ARCHIVE ISBN 1-58388-049-6
LOS ANGELES CITY FIRE APPARATUS 1953 - 1999 PHOTO ARCHIVE ISBN 1-58388-012-7
*MACK MODEL C FIRE TRUCKS 1957-1967 PHOTO ARCHIVE** ISBN 1-58388-014-3
*MACK MODEL L FIRE TRUCKS 1940-1954 PHOTO ARCHIVE** ISBN 1-882256-86-7
MAXIM FIRE APPARATUS 1914-1989 PHOTO ARCHIVE ISBN 1-58388-050-X
NAVY & MARINE CORPS FIRE APPARATUS 1836 -2000 PHOTO GALLERY ISBN 1-58388-031-3
POLICE CARS: RESTORING, COLLECTING & SHOWING AMERICA'S FINEST SEDANS ISBN 1-58388-046-1
SEAGRAVE 70TH ANNIVERSARY SERIES PHOTO ARCHIVE ISBN 1-58388-001-1
TASC FIRE APPARATUS 1946-1985 PHOTO ARCHIVE ISBN 1-58388-065-8
VOLUNTEER & RURAL FIRE APPARATUS PHOTO GALLERY ISBN 1-58388-005-4
W.S. DARLEY & CO. FIRE APPARATUS 1908-2000 PHOTO ARCHIVE ISBN 1-58388-061-5
WARD LAFRANCE FIRE TRUCKS 1918-1978 PHOTO ARCHIVE ISBN 1-58388-013-5
WILDLAND FIRE APPARATUS 1940-2001 PHOTO GALLERY ISBN 1-58388-056-9
YOUNG FIRE EQUIPMENT 1932-1991 PHOTO ARCHIVE ISBN 1-58388-015-1

RACING

CHAPARRAL CAN-AM RACING CARS FROM TEXAS LUDVIGSEN LIBRARY SERIES ISBN 1-58388-066-6
DRAG RACING FUNNY CARS OF THE 1970s PHOTO ARCHIVE ISBN 1-58388-068-2
EL MIRAGE IMPRESSIONS: DRY LAKES LAND SPEED RACING ISBN 1-58388-059-3
GT40 PHOTO ARCHIVE ISBN 1-882256-64-6
INDY CARS OF THE 1950s, LUDVIGSEN LIBRARY SERIES ISBN 1-58388-018-6
INDY CARS OF THE 1960s, LUDVIGSEN LIBRARY SERIES ISBN 1-58388-052-6
INDIANAPOLIS RACING CARS OF FRANK KURTIS 1941-1963 PHOTO ARCHIVE ISBN 1-58388-026-7
JUAN MANUEL FANGIO WORLD CHAMPION DRIVER SERIES PHOTO ALBUM ISBN 1-58388-008-9
LE MANS 1950 PHOTO ARCHIVE THE BRIGGS CUNNINGHAM CAMPAIGN ISBN 1-882256-21-2
MARIO ANDRETTI WORLD CHAMPION DRIVER SERIES PHOTO ALBUM ISBN 1-58388-009-7
MERCEDES-BENZ 300SL RACING CARS 1952-1953 LUDVIGSEN LIBRARY SERIES ISBN 1-58388-067-4
NOVI V-8 INDY CARS 1941-1965 LUDVIGSEN LIBRARY SERIES ISBN 1-58388-037-2
SEBRING 12-HOUR RACE 1970 PHOTO ARCHIVE ISBN 1-882256-20-4
VANDERBILT CUP RACE 1936 & 1937 PHOTO ARCHIVE ISBN 1-882256-66-2

RAILWAYS

CHICAGO, ST. PAUL, MINNEAPOLIS & OMAHA RAILWAY 1880-1940 PHOTO ARCHIVE ISBN 1-882256-67-0
CHICAGO & NORTH WESTERN RAILWAY 1975-1995 PHOTO ARCHIVE ISBN 1-882256-76-X
GREAT NORTHERN RAILWAY 1945-1970 PHOTO ARCHIVE ISBN 1-882256-56-5
GREAT NORTHERN RAILWAY 1945-1970 VOL 2 PHOTO ARCHIVE ISBN 1-882256-79-4
ILLINOIS CENTRAL RAILROAD 1854-1960 PHOTO ARCHIVE ISBN 1-58388-063-1
MILWAUKEE ROAD 1850-1960 PHOTO ARCHIVE ISBN 1-882256-61-1
MILWAUKEE ROAD DEPOTS 1856-1954 PHOTO ARCHIVE ISBN 1-58388-040-2
SHOW TRAINS OF THE 20TH CENTURY ISBN 1-58388-030-5
SOO LINE 1975-1992 PHOTO ARCHIVE ISBN 1-882256-68-9
TRAINS OF THE TWIN PORTS, DULUTH-SUPERIOR IN THE 1950s PHOTO ARCHIVE ISBN 1-58388-003-8
TRAINS OF THE CIRCUS 1872-1956 ISBN 1-58388-024-0
TRAINS of the UPPER MIDWEST PHOTO ARCHIVE STEAM&DIESEL in the1950S&1960S ISBN 1-58388-036-4
WISCONSIN CENTRAL LIMITED 1987-1996 PHOTO ARCHIVE ISBN 1-882256-75-1
WISCONSIN CENTRAL RAILWAY 1871-1909 PHOTO ARCHIVE ISBN 1-882256-78-6

TRUCKS

BEVERAGE TRUCKS 1910-1975 PHOTO ARCHIVE ISBN 1-882256-60-3
*BROCKWAY TRUCKS 1948-1961 PHOTO ARCHIVE** ISBN 1-882256-55-7
CHEVROLET EL CAMINO PHOTO HISTORY INCL GMC SPRINT & CABALLERO ISBN 1-58388-044-5
CIRCUS AND CARNIVAL TRUCKS 1923-2000 PHOTO ARCHIVE ISBN 1-58388-048-8
DODGE PICKUPS 1939-1978 PHOTO ALBUM ISBN 1-882256-82-4
DODGE POWER WAGONS 1940-1980 PHOTO ARCHIVE ISBN 1-882256-89-1
DODGE POWER WAGON PHOTO HISTORY ISBN 1-58388-019-4
DODGE RAM TRUCKS 1994-2001 PHOTO HISTORY ISBN 1-58388-051-8
DODGE TRUCKS 1929-1947 PHOTO ARCHIVE ISBN 1-882256-36-0
DODGE TRUCKS 1948-1960 PHOTO ARCHIVE ISBN 1-882256-37-9
FORD HEAVY-DUTY TRUCKS 1948-1998 PHOTO HISTORY ISBN 1-58388-043-7
JEEP 1941-2000 PHOTO ARCHIVE ISBN 1-58388-021-6
JEEP PROTOTYPES & CONCEPT VEHICLES PHOTO ARCHIVE ISBN 1-58388-033-X
LOGGING TRUCKS 1915-1970 PHOTO ARCHIVE ISBN 1-882256-59-X
*MACK MODEL AB PHOTO ARCHIVE** ISBN 1-882256-18-2
*MACK AP SUPER-DUTY TRUCKS 1926-1938 PHOTO ARCHIVE** ISBN 1-882256-54-9
*MACK MODEL B 1953-1966 VOL 1 PHOTO ARCHIVE** ISBN 1-882256-19-0
*MACK MODEL B 1953-1966 VOL 2 PHOTO ARCHIVE** ISBN 1-882256-34-4
*MACK EB-EC-ED-EE-EF-EG-DE 1936-1951 PHOTO ARCHIVE** ISBN 1-882256-29-8
*MACK EH-EJ-EM-EQ-ER-ES 1936-1950 PHOTO ARCHIVE** ISBN 1-882256-39-5
*MACK FC-FCSW-NW 1936-1947 PHOTO ARCHIVE** ISBN 1-882256-28-X
*MACK FG-FH-FJ-FK-FN-FP-FT-FW 1937-1950 PHOTO ARCHIVE** ISBN 1-882256-35-2
*MACK LF-LH-LJ-LM-LT 1940-1956 PHOTO ARCHIVE** ISBN 1-882256-38-7
*MACK TRUCKS PHOTO GALLERY** ISBN 1-882256-88-3
NEW CAR CARRIERS 1910-1998 PHOTO ALBUM ISBN 1-882256-98-0
PLYMOUTH COMMERCIAL VEHICLES PHOTO ARCHIVE ISBN 1-58388-004-6
REFUSE TRUCKS PHOTO ARCHIVE ISBN 1-58388-042-9
STUDEBAKER TRUCKS 1927-1940 PHOTO ARCHIVE ISBN 1-882256-40-9
STUDEBAKER TRUCKS 1941-1964 PHOTO ARCHIVE ISBN 1-882256-41-7
WHITE TRUCKS 1900-1937 PHOTO ARCHIVE ISBN 1-882256-80-8

TRACTORS & CONSTRUCTION EQUIPMENT

CASE TRACTORS 1912-1959 PHOTO ARCHIVE ISBN 1-882256-32-8
CATERPILLAR PHOTO GALLERY ISBN 1-882256-70-0
CATERPILLAR POCKET GUIDE THE TRACK-TYPE TRACTORS 1925-1957 ISBN 1-58388-022-4
CATERPILLAR D-2 & R-2 PHOTO ARCHIVE ISBN 1-882256-99-9
CATERPILLAR D-8 1933-1974 PHOTO ARCHIVE INCLUDING DIESEL 75 & RD-8 ISBN 1-882256-96-4
CATERPILLAR MILITARY TRACTORS VOLUME 1 PHOTO ARCHIVE ISBN 1-882256-16-6
CATERPILLAR MILITARY TRACTORS VOLUME 2 PHOTO ARCHIVE ISBN 1-882256-17-4
CATERPILLAR SIXTY PHOTO ARCHIVE ISBN 1-882256-05-0
CATERPILLAR TEN PHOTO ARCHIVE INCLUDING 7C FIFTEEN & HIGH FIFTEEN ISBN 1-58388-011-9
CATERPILLAR THIRTY PHOTO ARCHIVE 2ND ED. INC. BEST THIRTY, 6G THIRTY & R-4 ISBN 1-58388-006-2
CLETRAC AND OLIVER CRAWLERS PHOTO ARCHIVE ISBN 1-882256-43-3
CLASSIC AMERICAN STEAMROLLERS 1871-1935 PHOTO ARCHIVE ISBN 1-58388-038-0
FARMALL CUB PHOTO ARCHIVE ISBN 1-882256-71-9
FARMALL F- SERIES PHOTO ARCHIVE ISBN 1-882256-02-6
FARMALL MODEL H PHOTO ARCHIVE ISBN 1-882256-03-4
FARMALL MODEL M PHOTO ARCHIVE ISBN 1-882256-15-8
FARMALL REGULAR PHOTO ARCHIVE ISBN 1-882256-14-X
FARMALL SUPER SERIES PHOTO ARCHIVE ISBN 1-882256-49-2
FORDSON 1917-1928 PHOTO ARCHIVE ISBN 1-882256-33-6
HART-PARR PHOTO ARCHIVE ISBN 1-882256-08-5
HOLT TRACTORS PHOTO ARCHIVE ISBN 1-882256-10-7
INTERNATIONAL TRACTRACTOR PHOTO ARCHIVE ISBN 1-882256-48-4
INTERNATIONAL TD CRAWLERS 1933-1962 PHOTO ARCHIVE ISBN 1-882256-72-7
JOHN DEERE MODEL A PHOTO ARCHIVE ISBN 1-882256-12-3
JOHN DEERE MODEL B PHOTO ARCHIVE ISBN 1-882256-01-8
JOHN DEERE MODEL D PHOTO ARCHIVE ISBN 1-882256-00-X
JOHN DEERE 30 SERIES PHOTO ARCHIVE ISBN 1-882256-13-1
MARION CONSTRUCTION MACHINERY 1884 - 1975 PHOTO ARCHIVE ISBN 1-58388-060-7
MINNEAPOLIS-MOLINE U-SERIES PHOTO ARCHIVE ISBN 1-882256-07-7
OLIVER TRACTORS PHOTO ARCHIVE ISBN 1-882256-09-3
RUSSELL GRADERS PHOTO ARCHIVE ISBN 1-882256-11-5
TWIN CITY TRACTOR PHOTO ARCHIVE ISBN 1-882256-06-9

All Iconografix books are available from direct mail specialty book dealers and bookstores worldwide, or can be ordered from the publisher. For book trade and distribution information or to add your name to our mailing list and receive a **FREE CATALOG** contact:

Iconografix, PO Box 446, Hudson, Wisconsin, 54016 Telephone: (715) 381-9755, (800) 289-3504 (USA), Fax: (715) 381-9756

LE MANS 1950 PHOTO ARCHIVE
The Briggs Cunningham Campaign
Edited with introduction by Robert C. Auten • Photographs by Smith Hempstone Oliver

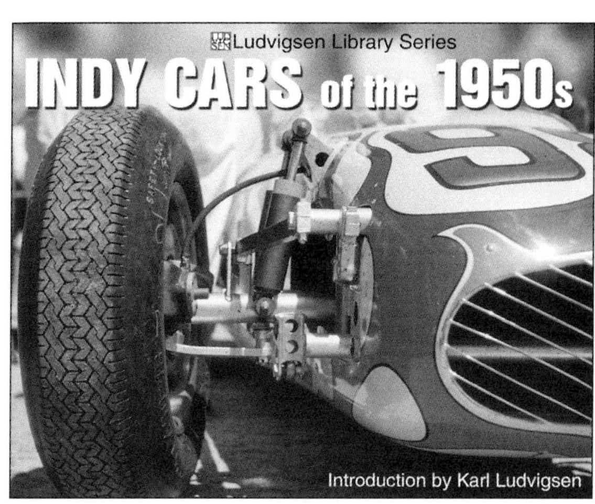

Ludvigsen Library Series
INDY CARS of the 1950s
Introduction by Karl Ludvigsen

INDIANAPOLIS RACING CARS
of FRANK KURTIS
1941 - 1963 PHOTO ARCHIVE
Gordon Eliot White

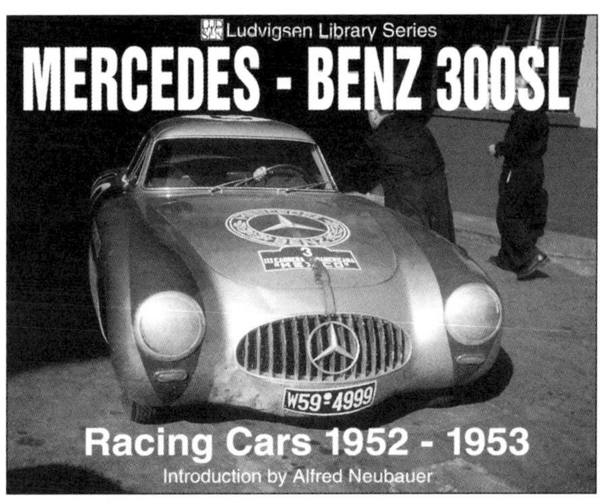

Ludvigsen Library Series
MERCEDES - BENZ 300SL
Racing Cars 1952 - 1953
Introduction by Alfred Neubauer

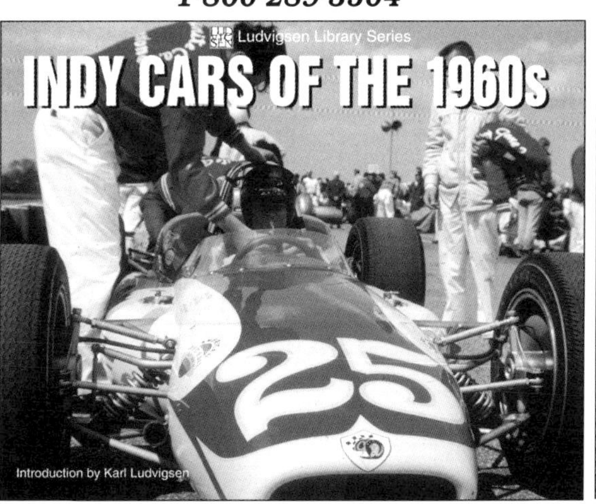

Ludvigsen Library Series
INDY CARS OF THE 1960s
Introduction by Karl Ludvigsen

Ludvigsen Library Series
NOVI V-8 INDY CARS
1941 - 1965
Introduction by Andy Granatelli

LUDVIGSEN LIBRARY LIMITED

The photographs in this book, supplied by the Ludvigsen Library, are available for purchase by enthusiasts. Based in London, this extensive automotive library, founded and owned by Karl Ludvigsen, is one of the world's most comprehensive sources of reference material about cars and the motor industry. Specializing in car and motor racing photography, it includes much rare and unpublished original material from John Dugdale, Edward Eves, Max Le Grand, Peter Keen, Karl Ludvigsen, Rodolfo Mailander, Ove Nielsen, Stanley Rosenthall and others.

All black and white prints are hand finished to museum display standards using the finest Ilford 1K fibre which gives a beautiful, durable finish that is perfect for mounting and display. Prints can be ordered from the Ludvigsen Library at the address below in three sizes at the following prices:

10 x 12	inches	US$40.00	UK£25.00
12 x 16	inches	US$55.00	UK£35.00
16 x 20	inches	US$75.00	UK£45.00

Please inquire concerning color, other sizes, and other subjects. Prices do not include packing and shipping fees, which will be advised in advance.

THE LUDVIGSEN LIBRARY LIMITED: 73 COLLIER STREET, LONDON N1 9BE, UNITED KINGDOM
TELEPHONE +44 (020) 7837 1700 FACSIMILE +44 (020) 7837 1776
E-MAIL LIBRARY@LUDVIGSEN.COM HTTP://WWW.LUDVIGSEN.COM